The Log Cabin Block
A Classic For Today's Quilts
Building Blocks Series 1 — Book 3

Special thanks to the following
for the beautiful fabrics used
in the quilts in this book:

Fine Lines Fabric
In The Beginning Fabrics
Northcott
Robert Kaufman Fabrics

All quilt designs by Sandy Boobar and
Sue Harvey of Pine Tree Country Quilts,
www.pinetreecountryquilts.com.

Published by

All American Crafts, Inc.
7 Waterloo Road
Stanhope, NJ 07874
www.allamericancrafts.com

Publisher | **Jerry Cohen**

Chief Executive Officer | **Darren Cohen**

Product Development
Director | **Brett Cohen**

Editor | **Sue Harvey**

Proofreader | **Natalie Rhinesmith**

Art Director | **Kelly Albertson**

Illustrations | **Kathleen Geary, Roni Palmisano
& Chrissy Scholz**

Product Development
Manager | **Pamela Mostek**

Vice President/Quilting Advertising
& Marketing | **Carol Newman**

Printed in China
ISBN:978-1-936708-07-9
UPC: 793573035301

www.allamericancrafts.com

Table of Contents

Welcome to the Building Blocks series of quilting books.

Whether you're making your first or your one hundred and first quilt, the eight books in this series will be an invaluable addition to your quilting library. Besides featuring the instructions for a different traditional and timeless block in each book, we've also included charts to give you all the quick information you need to change the block size for your own project.

Each book features complete instructions for three different quilts using the featured block with variations in size, color, and style—all designed to inspire you to use these timeless blocks for quilts with today's look.

The Finishing Basics section in each book gives you the tips and techniques you'll need to border, quilt, and bind the quilts in this book (or any quilt you may choose to make). If you're an experienced quilter, these books will be an excellent addition to your reference library. When you want to enlarge or reduce a block, the numbers are already there for you! No math required!

The blocks in the Building Blocks series of books have stood the test of time and are still favorites with quilters today. Although they're traditional blocks, they look very contemporary in today's bold and beautiful fabrics. This definitely puts them in the category of quilting classics!

For each block, you'll find a little background about its name, origin, or era, just to add a touch of quilting trivia. The block presented in this book is Log Cabin. It's safe to say that most quilters have made a Log Cabin quilt at one time or another. It is often the first quilt that new quilters try due to its simple construction.

Where and when the Log Cabin block originated is the subject of much discussion. The earliest known example in the United States is dated 1869. Early quilts were usually pieced on a fabric foundation. The strips were often narrow scraps. The center square of the block was red with light strips on one side and dark strips on the other side. Common folklore explains the colors of the block: the red is the hearth of the home, the light side represents sunshine, and the dark side is shadow.

The Log Cabin block appeals to quilters today just as much as it did to quilters 200 years ago. It has been twisted and turned, stretched and miniaturized, foundation-pieced and strip-pieced, but the challenge to find the next variation lives on. Give the quilts in this book a try; but be forewarned, Log Cabin quilts have proven to be addictive!

Log Cabin

se these instructions to make the blocks for the quilts in this book. The materials needed for each quilt and the cutting instructions are given with the pattern for the quilt. Also included is a Build It Your Way chart with four different sizes for this block and the sizes to cut the pieces for one block. Use this information to design your own quilt or to change the size of any of the quilts in this book.

BUILDING THE BLOCK
Use a ¹/₄" seam allowance throughout.

1. Sew a B strip to one side of the A center. Press seam toward the B strip.

2. Stitch a C strip to the left edge of the center unit. Press seam toward the C strip.

3. Sew a D strip to the bottom of the center unit. Press seam toward the D strip.

Build It Better

Save time and trips to the ironing board! Chain-piece all of the same strip to the block centers, then snip them apart. Press them all at once. Then chain-piece all of the next strip.

4. Stitch an E strip to the right edge of the center unit to complete the first round of strips. Press seam toward the E strip.

5. Sew F, G, H, and I strips around the center unit in the same counterclockwise manner to complete the second round of strips. Press seams away from the center unit as each strip is added.

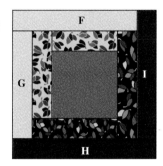

6. Stitch J, K, L, and M strips around the center unit in the same counterclockwise manner to complete the third round of strips and to complete the block. Press seams away from the center unit as each strip is added.

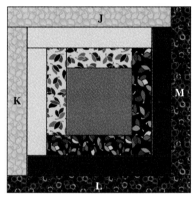

Build It Better

Need a quick gift or holiday accent? Make four 16" or 20" blocks, sew together, add quilting, and bind. Presto–instant topper or wall quilt!

7. Repeat to complete the number of blocks needed for the quilt that you have chosen.

Build It Your Way

Piece	8" Block	12" Block	16" Block	20" Block
A	2¹/2" x 2¹/2"	3¹/2" x 3¹/2"	4¹/2" x 4¹/2"	5¹/2" x 5¹/2"
B	1¹/2" x 2¹/2"	2" x 3¹/2"	2¹/2" x 4¹/2"	3" x 5¹/2"
C, D	1¹/2" x 3¹/2"	2" x 5"	2¹/2" x 6¹/2"	3" x 8"
E, F	1¹/2" x 4¹/2"	2" x 6¹/2"	2¹/2" x 8¹/2"	3" x 10¹/2"
G, H	1¹/2" x 5¹/2"	2" x 8"	2¹/2" x 10¹/2"	3" x 13"
I, J	1¹/2" x 6¹/2"	2" x 9¹/2"	2¹/2" x 12¹/2"	3" x 15¹/2"
K, L	1¹/2" x 7¹/2"	2" x 11"	2¹/2" x 14¹/2"	3" x 18"
M	1¹/2" x 8¹/2"	2" x 12¹/2"	2¹/2" x 16¹/2"	3" x 20¹/2"

Heat Wave

Bright hot fabrics on one side and cool dark fabrics on the other side make these Log Cabin blocks sizzle. The blocks are arranged in the most popular Log Cabin design, Barn Raising. This quilt brings to mind "heat" shimmering off hot pavement on a blistering summer day.

Finished Quilt Size: 44" x 60"
Finished Block Size: 8" x 8"
Number of Blocks: 24
Skill Level: Beginner

MATERIALS
All yardages are based on 42"-wide fabric.

- ❖ $1/2$ yard of orange texture
- ❖ $1/3$ yard of gold leaf print
- ❖ $3/8$ yard of black leaf print
- ❖ $1/2$ yard of yellow texture
- ❖ 1 yard of purple texture
- ❖ $1/2$ yard of gold texture
- ❖ $5/8$ yard of black circle print
- ❖ 1 yard of multicolor geometric print
- ❖ 4 yards of backing fabric
- ❖ 52" x 68" piece of batting
- ❖ Thread to match fabrics
- ❖ Rotary cutting tools
- ❖ Basic sewing supplies

CUTTING

Label all pieces with the letters assigned. They will be used throughout the instructions.

From the orange texture, cut
- 2 strips 2¹/₂" x 42"; recut into (24) 2¹/₂" A squares
- 4 strips 1¹/₂" x 42" for inner border

From the gold leaf print, cut
- 4 strips 1¹/₂" x 42"; recut into (24) 1¹/₂" x 2¹/₂" B strips and (24) 1¹/₂" x 3¹/₂" C strips

From the black leaf print, cut
- 5 strips 1¹/₂" x 42"; recut into (24) 1¹/₂" x 3¹/₂" D strips and (24) 1¹/₂" x 4¹/₂" E strips

From the yellow texture, cut
- 7 strips 1¹/₂" x 42"; recut into (24) 1¹/₂" x 4¹/₂" F strips and (24) 1¹/₂" x 5¹/₂" G strips

From the purple texture, cut
- 8 strips 1¹/₂" x 42"; recut into (24) 1¹/₂" x 5¹/₂" H strips and (24) 1¹/₂" x 6¹/₂" I strips
- 6 strips 2¹/₄" x 42" for binding

From the gold texture, cut
- 9 strips 1¹/₂" x 42"; recut into (24) 1¹/₂" x 6¹/₂" J strips and (24) 1¹/₂" x 7¹/₂" K strips

From the black circle print, cut
- 11 strips 1¹/₂" x 42"; recut into (24) 1¹/₂" x 7¹/₂" L strips and (24) 1¹/₂" x 8¹/₂" M strips

From the multicolor geometric print, cut
- 5 strips 5¹/₂" x 42" for outer border

From the backing fabric, cut
- 2 pieces 68" long

MAKING THE LOG CABIN BLOCKS

Use a ¹/₄" seam allowance throughout unless otherwise instructed.

1. Refer to Building the Block on page 6 to make (24) 8¹/₂" x 8¹/₂" Log Cabin blocks.

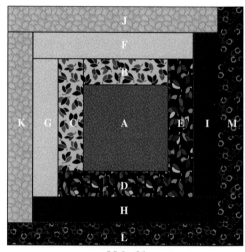

Make 24

COMPLETING THE TOP

1. Sew four blocks together to make row 1. Press seams to the left. Repeat to make rows 3, 4, and 6.

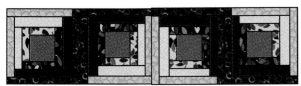

Make 4 – Rows 1, 3, 4, and 6

2. Sew four blocks together to make row 2. Press seams to the right. Repeat to make row 5.

Make 4 – Rows 2 and 5

3. Sew the block rows together to complete the 32 1/2" x 48 1/2" quilt center, carefully turning the rows to make the quilt design. Press seams in one direction. (See the Quilt Assembly Diagram on page 12.)

4. Sew the four 1 1/2" x 42" red texture strips short ends together to make a long strip. Press seams in one direction. Cut into two 48 1/2" strips and two 34 1/2" strips. Sew the longer strips to the long sides and the shorter strips to the top and bottom of the quilt center. Press seams toward the strips. ***Note: Refer to Finishing Basics on page 26 for Information about cutting border strips.***

5. Sew the five 5 1/2" x 42" multicolor geometric print strips short ends together to make a long strip. Press seams in one direction. Cut into two 50 1/2" strips and two 44 1/2" strips. Sew the longer strips to the long sides and the shorter strips to the top and bottom to complete the quilt top. Press seams toward the strips.

FINISHING THE QUILT

1. Remove the selvage edges from the backing pieces. Sew the pieces together down the length with a 1/2" seam allowance. Trim the sides to make a 52" x 68" backing piece. Press seam open.

2. Refer to Finishing Basics to layer, quilt, and bind your quilt.

Build It Better

Need two quilts? The sharp contrast between the light and dark sides of the blocks in this quilt makes it perfect for the traditional Sunshine and Shadow arrangement. Just turn the blocks so the light sides meet and the dark sides meet in the block rows when the rows are joined. A whole new look!

Quilt Assembly Diagram

This quilt uses the same hot yellow and sharp contrast between light and dark, but the use of a lot of prints blurs the edges between the strips. The result—a more sophisticated quilt with a lacy effect created by the blocks.

Wildfire

Another HOT quilt—this one with a little cool blue thrown in for temperature control! This one uses the classic Fields and Furrows arrangement for the blocks to create the diagonal swaths of color. Small rectangular blocks in the border continue the flow of color across the plain border right out to the edges of the quilt.

Finished Quilt Size: 64" x 76"
Finished Block Size: 12" x 12" and 6" x 8"
Number of Blocks: 20 and 18
Skill Level: Intermediate

MATERIALS
All yardages are based on 42"-wide fabric.

- $1^5/_8$ yards of rust print
- $2^1/_4$ yards of dark blue print
- $^1/_2$ yard of yellow/orange print
- $1^1/_8$ yards of light blue/yellow print
- $^7/_8$ yard of orange print
- 1 yard of medium blue print
- 5 yards of backing fabric
- 72" x 84" piece of batting
- Thread to match fabrics
- Template material
- Rotary cutting tools
- Basic sewing supplies

CUTTING

Label all pieces with the letters assigned. They will be used throughout the instructions. All pieces that include a letter and 1 are for the square blocks; pieces with a letter and 2 are for the rectangular blocks.

From the rust print, cut

- 1 strip $3^7/8$" x 42"; recut into (10) $3^7/8$" squares, then cut each square in half diagonally to make 20 A1 triangles
- 1 strip $9^1/2$" x 42"; recut into (20) 2" x $9^1/2$" J1 strips
- 1 strip 11" x 42"; recut into (20) 2" x 11" K1 strips
- 1 strip $6^1/2$" x 42"; recut into (18) $1^1/4$" x $6^1/2$" J2 strips
- 1 strip $5^3/4$" x 42"; recut into (18) $1^1/2$" x $5^3/4$" K2 strips
- 2 strips $6^1/2$" x 42"; recut into (4) $6^1/2$" N squares and (4) $7^1/2$" x $6^1/2$" P rectangles

From the dark blue print, cut

- 1 strip $3^7/8$" x 42"; recut into (10) $3^7/8$" squares, then cut each square in half diagonally to make 20 A1 triangles
- 1 strip 11" x 42"; recut into (20) 2" x 11" L1 strips
- 1 strip $12^1/2$" x 42" recut into (20) 2" x $12^1/2$" M1 strips
- 1 strip $7^1/2$" x 42"; recut into (18) $1^1/4$" x $7^1/2$" L2 strips
- 1 strip $6^1/2$" x 42"; recut into (18) $1^1/2$" x $6^1/2$" M2 strips
- 2 strips $6^1/2$" x 42"; recut into (10) $6^1/2$" O squares
- 7 strips $2^1/4$" x 42" for binding

From the yellow/orange print, cut

- 1 strip $3^1/2$" x 42"; recut into (20) 2" x $3^1/2$" B1 strips
- 1 strip 5" x 42"; recut into (20) 2" x 5" C1 strips
- 1 strip $2^1/2$" x 42"; recut into (18) $1^1/4$" x $2^1/2$" B2 strips
- 1 strip $2^3/4$" x 42"; recut into (18) $1^1/2$" x $2^3/4$" C2 strips

From the light blue/yellow print, cut

- 1 strip 5" x 42"; recut into (20) 2" x 5" D1 strips
- 1 strip $6^1/2$" x 42"; recut into (20) 2" x $6^1/2$" E1 strips
- 1 strip $3^1/2$" x 42"; recut into (18) $1^1/4$" x $3^1/2$" D2 strips
- 1 strip $3^1/2$" x 42"; recut into (18) $1^1/2$" x $3^1/2$" E2 strips
- 6 strips $2^1/2$" x 42" for inner border

From the orange print, cut

- 1 strip $6^1/2$" x 42"; recut into (20) 2" x $6^1/2$" F1 strips
- 1 strip 8" x 42"; recut into (20) 2" x 8" G1 strips
- 1 strip $4^1/2$" x 42"; recut into (18) $1^1/4$" x $4^1/2$" F2 strips
- 1 strip $4^1/4$" x 42"; recut into (18) $1^1/2$" x $4^1/4$" G2 strips

From the medium blue print, cut

- 1 strip 8" x 42"; recut into (20) 2" x 8" H1 strips
- 1 strip $9^1/2$" x 42"; recut into (20) 2" x $9^1/2$" I1 strips
- 1 strip $5^1/2$" x 42"; recut into (18) $1^1/4$" x $5^1/2$" H2 strips
- 1 strip 5" x 42"; recut into (18) $1^1/2$" x 5" I2 strips

From the backing fabric, cut

- 2 pieces 84" long

MAKING THE LOG CABIN BLOCKS

Use a $1/4$" seam allowance throughout unless otherwise instructed.

1. Sew a rust A1 triangle to a dark blue A1 triangle to make an A1 square. Press seam to the dark blue side. Repeat to make 20 A1 squares total.

Make 20

2. Refer to Building the Block on page 6 to make (20) 12¹/₂" x 12¹/₂" Log Cabin blocks using the A1 squares and B1-M1 fabric strips. Always sew the yellow/orange/rust strips to the rust sides of the A1 center square and the blue strips to the dark blue sides of the A1 center square.

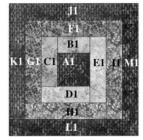

Make 20

3. Prepare a template for the A2 piece using the full-size pattern on page 18.

4. Cut eight rust print A2 pieces and eight dark blue A2 pieces. Flip the template over and cut 10 reversed rust print A2 pieces and 10 reversed dark blue A2 pieces.

Make 8

5. Sew a rust A2 piece to a dark blue A2 piece to make an A2 center rectangle. Press seam to the dark blue side. Repeat to make eight A2 center rectangles total. Repeat with the reversed A2 rust and dark blue pieces to make 10 reversed A2 center rectangles.

Make 10

6. Refer to Building the Block on page 6 to make eight 6¹/₂" x 8¹/₂" Log Cabin rectangular blocks using the A2 center rectangles and B2-M2 strips.

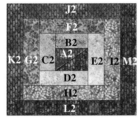

Make 8

7. Refer to Building the Block on page 6 to make (10) 6¹/₂" x 8¹/₂" reversed Log Cabin rectangular blocks using the reversed A2 center rectangles and B2-M2 strips. Be very careful to sew the strips clockwise around the center rectangle for these blocks.

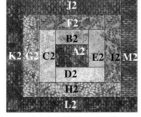

Make 10 Reversed

COMPLETING THE TOP

1. Sew four blocks together to make an X row. Press seams to the left. Repeat to make three X rows total.

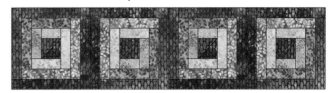

X Row – Make 3

2. Sew four blocks together to make a Y row. Press seams to the right. Repeat to make two Y rows total.

Y Row – Make 2

3. Sew the block rows together to complete the 48¹/₂" x 60¹/₂" quilt center, carefully turning the rows to make the quilt design. Press seams in one direction. (See the Quilt Assembly Diagram on page 18.)

4. Sew the 2¹/₂" x 42" light blue/yellow print strips short ends together to make a long strip. Press seams in one direction. Cut into two 60¹/₂" strips and two 52¹/₂" strips. Sew the longer strips to the long sides and the shorter strips to the top and bottom of the quilt center. Press seams toward the strips. *Note: Refer to Finishing Basics on page 26 for information about cutting border strips.*

5. Join five reversed Log Cabin rectangular blocks with two rust N squares and two dark blue O squares to make a side border strip. Press seams toward the N and O squares. Repeat to make a second border strip.

Side border – Make 2

6. Sew the border strips to the long sides of the quilt center. Press seams toward the light blue/yellow border.

7. Join four Log Cabin rectangular blocks with two rust P rectangles and three dark blue O squares to make the top border strip. Press seams toward the O squares and P rectangles. Repeat to make the bottom border strip.

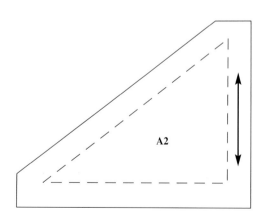

Top/Bottom border – Make 2

8. Sew the border strips to the top and bottom of the quilt center to complete the quilt top. Press seams toward the light blue/yellow border.

FINISHING THE QUILT

1. Remove the selvage edges from the backing pieces. Sew the pieces together down the length with a 1/2" seam allowance. Trim the sides to make a 72" x 84" backing piece. Press seam open.

2. Refer to Finishing Basics to layer, quilt, and bind your quilt.

A2

Build It Better

Lots of different strips everywhere? Get them under control with zipper-top plastic bags and masking tape. For each different lettered strip, cut a piece of masking tape, put it on a plastic bag, and write the letter/number ID on the tape. The strips stay together until you need them. And the bags are reusable–just peel off the tape and add a new piece for the next project!

Quilt Assembly Diagram

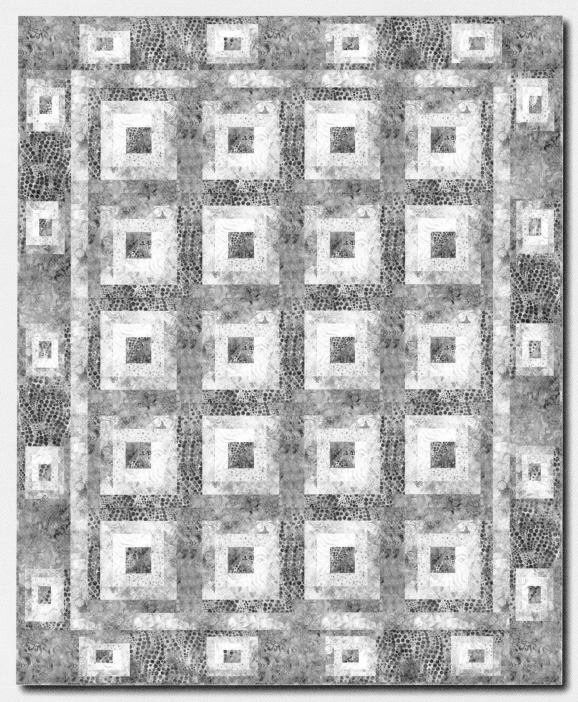

Where the original quilt is fiery, stark, and makes you think of Mother Nature's temper, this quilt introduces you to her softer, feminine side. Despite the different 'feel' of these quilts, notice that in both cases, the cooler fabrics in blue and green take a supporting role to the hotter pink and orange. Temperature plays a part in more than just the weather!

Watercolor Garden

Blur and blend the edges of the blocks and fabrics to look like brushstrokes of watery, wavy color against color.
Log Cabin half-triangles and stripe corner triangles continue the colors and pattern right out to the borders.

Finished Quilt Size: 64" x 64"
Finished Block Size: 12" x 12"
Number of Blocks: 13
Skill Level: Intermediate

MATERIALS
All yardages are based on 42"-wide fabric.

- ❖ $1^1/_3$ yards of multicolor stripe
- ❖ $3/_8$ yard of light aqua print
- ❖ $5/_8$ yard of lilac flower print
- ❖ $1/_2$ yard of bright turquoise mottled
- ❖ $7/_8$ yard of medium purple print
- ❖ $3/_4$ yard of dark turquoise print
- ❖ $1^1/_4$ yards of dark purple print
- ❖ $1^1/_8$ yards of multicolor floral
- ❖ $4^1/_4$ yards of backing fabric
- ❖ 72" x 72" piece of batting
- ❖ Thread to match fabrics
- ❖ Spray starch
- ❖ Rotary cutting tools
- ❖ Rotary ruler with a 45˚ line
- ❖ Basic sewing supplies

CUTTING

Label all pieces with the letters assigned. They will be used throughout the instructions.

From the multicolor stripe, cut

- 2 strips 3$1/2$" x 42"; recut into (13) 3$1/2$" A squares and (4) 2$5/8$" AA squares
- 1 strip 5$1/2$" x 42"; recut into (2) 5$1/2$" squares, then cut each square twice diagonally to make 8 N triangles
- 6 strips 2" x 42" for inner border
- 7 strips 2$1/4$" x 42" for binding

From the light aqua print, cut

- 5 strips 2" x 42"; recut into (13) 2" x 5" D strips, (13) 2" x 6$1/2$" E strips, and (4) 2" x 7$1/2$" U strips

From the lilac flower print, cut

- 5 strips 2" x 42"; recut into (13) 2" x 3$1/2$" B strips, (13) 2" x 5" C strips, (8) 2" x 6" O strips, and (4) 2" x 7$1/2$" P strips
- 1 strip 4$3/4$" x 42"; recut into (4) 4$3/4$" Z squares

From the bright turquoise mottled, cut

- 7 strips 2" x 42"; recut into (13) 2" x 8" H strips, (13) 2" x 9$1/2$" I strips, and (4) 2" x 10$1/2$" V strips

From the medium purple print, cut

- 8 strips 2" x 42"; recut into (13) 2" x 6$1/2$" F strips, (13) 2" x 8" G strips, (8) 2" x 9" Q strips, and (4) 2" x 10$1/2$" R strips
- 1 strip 6$7/8$" x 42"; recut into (4) 6$7/8$" Y squares

From the dark turquoise print, cut

- 12 strips 2" x 42"; recut into (13) 2" x 11" L strips, (13) 2" x 12$1/2$" M strips, and (4) 2" x 13$1/2$" W strips

From the dark purple print, cut

- 12 strips 2" x 42"; recut into (13) 2" x 9$1/2$" J strips, (13) 2" x 11" K strips, (8) 2" x 12" S strips, and (4) 2" x 13$1/2$" T strips
- 1 strip 9$3/8$" x 42"; recut into (2) 9$3/8$" X squares

From the multicolor floral, cut

- 6 strips 5$1/2$" x 42" for outer border

From the backing fabric, cut

- 2 pieces 72" long

MAKING THE LOG CABIN BLOCKS

Use a 1/4" seam allowance throughout unless otherwise instructed.

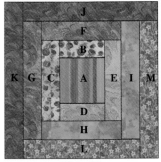

Make 13

1. Refer to Building the Block on page 6 to make (13) 12$1/2$" x 12$1/2$" Log Cabin blocks.

MAKING THE SETTING TRIANGLES

1. Sew a lilac O strip to the left short edge of a stripe N triangle, aligning one end of the strip with the square corner of the triangle. Press seam toward the O strip to complete one NO unit.

2. Sew a lilac P strip to the remaining short edge of the N triangle, aligning one end of the strip with the square corner of the NO unit. Press seam toward the P strip.

3. Repeat with medium purple Q and R strips and dark purple S and T strips. Apply a heavy coat of spray starch to the wrong side of the stitched unit and press dry. This will help to stabilize the long edge after the ends have been trimmed in the next step.

4. Trim the ends of the strips even with the edge of the N triangle, placing the 45° line of the ruler on one of the seams or the outside edge of the pieced unit. Handle the completed triangles carefully.

5. Repeat to make four side triangles total.

6. Repeat steps 1–4 to make two top/bottom triangles, placing O, Q, and S strips on the left edge of the N triangles and U, V, and W strips on the right edge of the N triangles.

7. Repeat steps 1–4 to make two reversed top/bottom triangles, placing U, V, and W strips on the left edge of the N triangles and O, Q, and S strips on the right edge of the N triangles.

8. Mark a diagonal line on the wrong side of each medium purple Y square, lilac Z square, and stripe AA square.

9. Place a Y square right sides together on one corner of each dark purple X square. Stitch on the marked line. Trim the seam allowances to 1/4". Press the Y corners to the right side. Repeat on the opposite corner of the X squares.

45° line

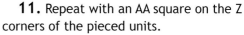

Trim

Side – Make 4

Top/Bottom – Make 2

Reversed Top/Bottom – Make 2

10. Repeat with a Z square on the Y corners of the pieced units.

11. Repeat with an AA square on the Z corners of the pieced units.

12. Cut each pieced unit diagonally in half from corner to corner of the dark purple center section to make four corner triangles.

COMPLETING THE TOP

1. Join the blocks in five diagonal rows with the pieced side triangles (ST) and the pieced top/bottom (TB) and reversed top/bottom (TB-R) triangles. Press seams in opposite directions from row to row. Be very careful handling and pressing the pieced triangles to avoid stretching the long bias edges. (Refer to the Quilt Assembly Diagram on page 24.)

2. Sew the rows together and add a corner triangle to each angled edge to complete the 51½" x 51½" quilt center. Press seams in one direction and toward the corner triangles.

3. Stitch the 2" x 42" multicolor stripe strips short ends together to make a long strip. Press seams in one direction. Cut into two 51½" strips and two 54½" strips. Sew the shorter strips to opposite sides and the longer strips to the remaining sides of the quilt center. Press seams toward the strips. *Note: Refer to the Finishing Basics on page 26 for information about cutting border strips.*

4. Sew the 5½" x 42" multicolor floral strips short ends together to make a long strip. Press seams in one direction. Cut into two 54½" strips and two 64½"

strips. Sew the shorter strips to opposite sides and the longer strips to the remaining sides to complete the quilt top. Press seams toward the strips.

FINISHING THE QUILT

1. Remove the selvage edges from the backing pieces. Sew the pieces together down the length with a $1/2$" seam allowance. Trim the sides to make a 72" x 72" backing piece. Press seam open.

2. Refer to Finishing Basics to layer, quilt, and bind your quilt.

Build It Better

Don't let diagonal rows make you dizzy! Mark the row numbers on small pieces of paper and pin them to the top piece in each row. It's a snap to keep track of the layout and the order of the blocks in the rows.

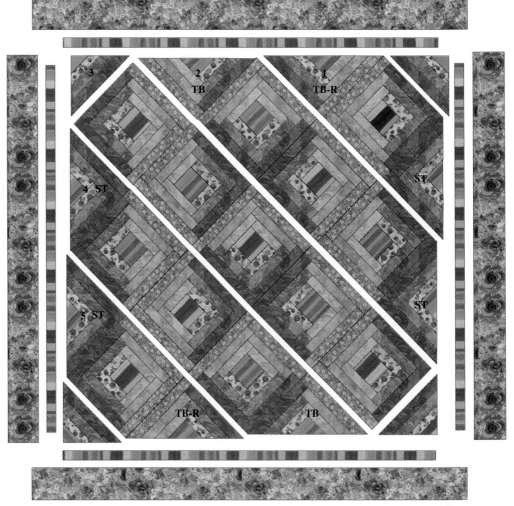

Quilt Assembly Diagram

The colorful garden of the original quilt is transformed into a winter garden of evergreens, snow, and ice.
The soft flowing lines have changed into distinctive angular lines with the use of more solid fabrics in the blocks.

Finishing Basics

ADDING BORDERS

Borders are an important part of your quilt. They add another design element, and act much like a picture frame to complement and support the center.

There are two basic types of borders—butted corners and mitered corners. Butted corners are the most common. For this technique, border strips are stitched to opposite sides of the quilt center, pressed, and then strips are sewn to the remaining sides. Mitered corners are often used to continue a pattern around the corners; for example, the stripe in a fabric or a pieced border design.

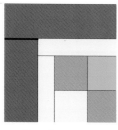 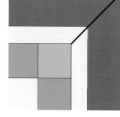

Butted corners   **Mitered corners**

Lengths are given for the borders in the individual quilt instructions. In most cases, fabric-width strips are joined to make a strip long enough to cut two side strips and top and bottom strips. Because of differences in piecing and pressing, your quilt center may differ slightly in size from the mathematically exact size used to determine the border lengths. Before cutting the strips for butted corners, refer to the instructions given here to measure for lengths to fit your quilt center. For mitered borders, extra length is already included in the sizes given in the instructions to make it easier to stitch the miters. It should be enough to allow for any overall size differences.

BUTTED CORNERS

1. Press the quilt center. Arrange it on a flat surface with the edges straight.

2. Fold the quilt in half lengthwise, matching edges and corners. Finger-press the center fold to make a crease. Unfold.

3. Measure along the center ceased line to determine the length of the quilt center.

 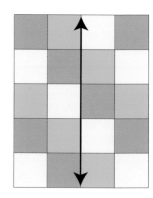

Fold in half

4. Cut two strips this length.

5. Fold the strips in half across the width and finger-press to make a crease.

6. Place a strip right sides together on one long edge of the quilt center, aligning the creased center of the strip with the center of the long edge. Pin in place at the center. Align the ends of the strips with the top and bottom edges of the quilt center. Pin in place at each end.

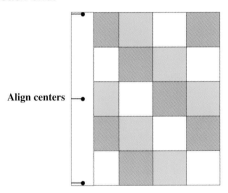

Align centers

7. Pin between the ends and center, easing any fullness, if necessary.

8. Stitch the border to the quilt center. Press.

9. Repeat on the remaining long edge.

10. Fold the quilt in half across the width and crease to mark the center. Unfold. Measure along the creased line to determine the width of the bordered quilt center.

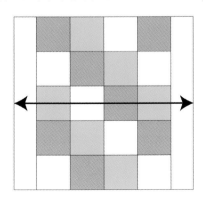

11. Cut two strips this length.

12. Repeat steps 5–9 on the top and bottom edges of the quilt center.

MITERED CORNERS

1. Prepare the border strips as directed in the individual pattern.

2. Make a mark 1/4" on each side of the quilt corners.

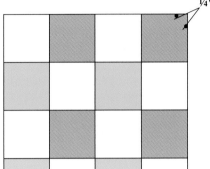

1/4"

3. Center the border strips on each side of the quilt top and pin in place. Stitch in place, stopping and locking stitches at the 1/4" mark at each corner.

4. Fold the quilt top in half diagonally with wrong sides together. Arrange two border ends right sides together.

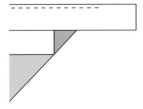

5. Mark a 45° angle line from the locked stitching on the border to the outside edge of the border.

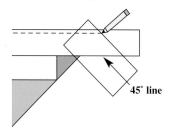

45° line

6. Stitch on the marked line, starting exactly at the locked stitch. Trim seam allowance to 1/4".

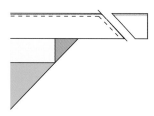

7. Press the mitered corner seam open and the seam between the border and the rest of the quilt toward the border.

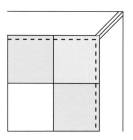

8. Repeat these steps on each corner of the quilt.

LAYERING, BASTING & QUILTING

You may choose to do your own quilting or take your projects to a machine quilter. Be sure that your backing and batting are at least 4" wider and 4" longer on each side of the quilt top. The size needed is given in the Materials list for each project.

If you would like to quilt your own project, there are many good books about hand and machine quilting. Check with your quilting friends or at your local quilt shop for recommendations. Here are the basic steps to do your own quilting:

1. Mark the quilt top with a quilting design, if desired.

2. Place the backing right side down on a flat surface. Place the batting on top. Center the quilt top right side up on top of the batting. Smooth all the layers. Thread-baste, pin, or spray-baste the layers together to hold while quilting.

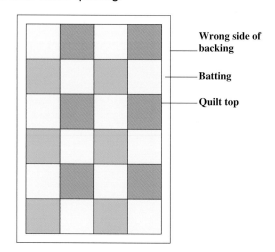

Wrong side of backing

Batting

Quilt top

3. Quilt the layers by hand or machine.

4. When quilting is finished, trim the batting and backing even with the quilted top.

BINDING

The patterns in this book include plenty of fabric to cut either 2¼" or 2½" wide strips for straight-grain, double-fold binding. In some cases, a wider binding or bias binding is needed because of a specific edge treatment; extra yardage is included when necessary.

PREPARING STRAIGHT-GRAIN, DOUBLE-FOLD BINDING

1. Cut strips as directed for the individual pattern. Remove selvage edges.

2. Place the ends of two binding strips right sides together at a right angle. Mark a line from inside corner to inside corner. Stitch on the marked line. Trim seam allowance to ¼".

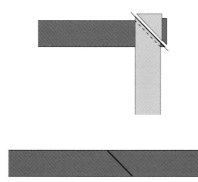

3. Repeat step 2 to join all binding strips into one long strip. Press seams to one side. Fold the strip in half lengthwise with wrong sides together and press.

PREPARING DOUBLE-FOLD BIAS BINDING

1. Cut an 18" x 42" strip from the binding fabric.

2. Place the 45° angle line of a rotary ruler on one edge of the strip. Trim off one corner of the strip.

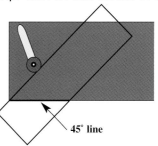

45° line

3. Cut binding strips in the width specified in the pattern from the angled end of the strip.

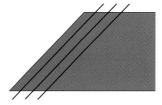

4. Each strip will be approximately 25" long. Cut strips to total the length needed for the pattern, repeating steps 1 and 2 if needed.

5. Align the ends of two strips with right sides together. Stitch ¼" from the ends.

6. Repeat to join all binding strips into one long strip. Press seams to one side.

ADDING THE BINDING

1. Leaving a 6"-8" tail and beginning several inches from a corner, align the raw edges of the binding with the edge of the quilt. Stitch along the edge with a 1/4" seam allowance, locking stitches at the beginning.

2. Stop 1/4" from the first corner and lock stitching. Remove the quilt from your machine. Turn the quilt so the next edge is to your right. Fold the binding end up and then back down so the fold is aligned with the previous edge of the quilt and the binding is aligned with the edge to your right. Starting at the edge of the quilt, stitch the binding to the next corner.

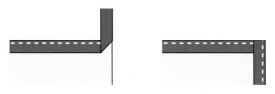

3. Repeat step 2 to attach binding to the rest of the quilt, stopping stitching 6"–8" from the starting point and locking stitches.

4. Unfold the ends of the strips. Press flat. About halfway between the stitched ends, fold the beginning strip up at a right angle. Press. Fold the ending strip down at a right angle, with the folded edge butted against the fold of the beginning end. Press.

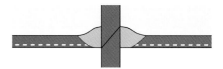

5. Trim each end 1/4" from creased fold. Place the trimmed ends right sides together. Pin to hold. Stitch 1/4" from the ends. Press the seam allowance open.

6. Refold the strip in half. Press. Arrange the strip on the edge of the quilt and stitch in place to finish the binding.

7. Fold the edge of the binding over the raw edges to the back of the quilt. Hand stitch in place, covering the machine stitches and mitering the corners.

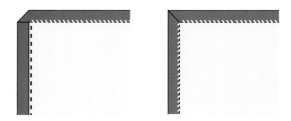